READING/WRITING
COMPANION

Mc
Graw
Hill
Education

Cover: Nathan Love, Erwin Madrid

mheducation.com/prek-12

Copyright © McGraw-Hill Education

All rights reserved. No part of this publication may be
reproduced or distributed in any form or by any means,
or stored in a database or retrieval system, without the
prior written consent of McGraw-Hill Education,
including, but not limited to, network storage or
transmission, or broadcast for distance learning.

Send all inquiries to:
McGraw-Hill Education
Two Penn Plaza
New York, NY 10121

ISBN: 978-0-07-901797-0
MHID: 0-07-901797-5

Printed in the United States of America.

11 LMN 23   C

Welcome to Wonders!

Read exciting **Literature**, **Science**, and **Social Studies** texts!

★ **LEARN** about the world around you!

★ **THINK**, **SPEAK**, and **WRITE** about genres!

★ **COLLABORATE** in discussions and inquiry!

★ **EXPRESS** yourself!

my.mheducation.com

Use your student login to read texts and practice phonics, spelling, grammar, and more!

Unit 4 Animals Everywhere

The Big Idea

Week 1 • Animal Features

 Digital Tools Find this eBook and other resources at: my.mheducation.com

Week 2 • Animals Together

Week 3 • In the Wild

Week 4 • Insects!

Week 5 • Working with Animals

Writing and Grammar

Wrap Up the Unit

SOCIAL STUDIES

SCIENCE

Unit 4
Animals Everywhere

MIYAKO/a.collectionRF/Getty Images

Listen to and think about the poem "Animals on the Go."

 Talk about other animals you know. How do they move?

The Big Idea

What animals do you know about?
What are they like?

Talk About It

? Essential Question How do animals' bodies help them?

Talk about these giraffes. How do their necks help them eat?

Write what you know about giraffes. Compare them to another animal you know.

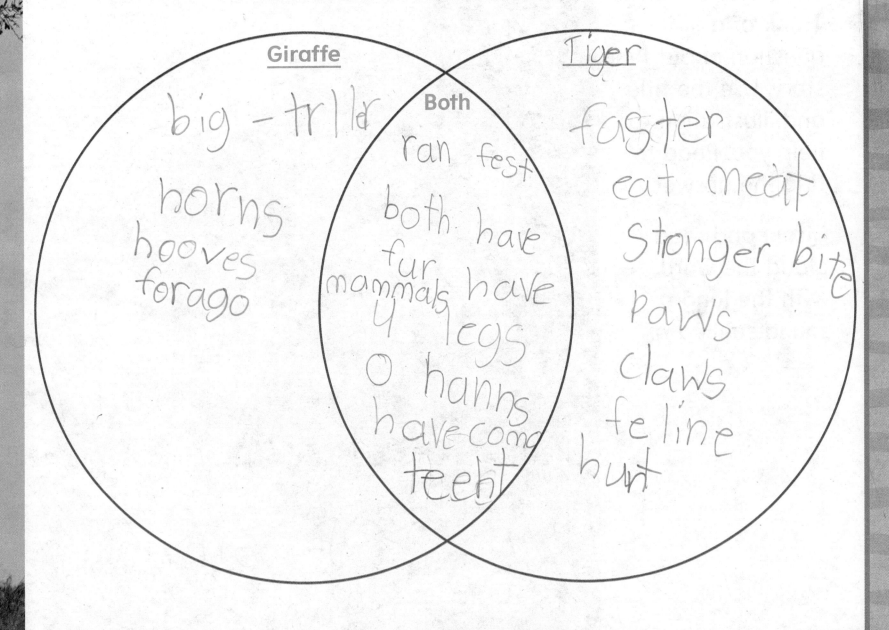

Giraffe

Tiger

Both

big - trllr

horns

hooves

forago

ran fest

both have

fur

mammals have

4 legs

O hanns

have coma

teeht

faster

eat meat

stonger bite

paws

claws

feline

hunt

Shared Read

🔍 **Find Text Evidence**

Think of a question about the story. Use the title and illustration to help you. Read to find the answer.

✏️ **Circle** and read aloud the word with the long *a* sound spelled *ai*.

Essential Question

? How do animals' bodies help them?

Snail and Frog Race

not real
long time
story
fak - fiction

Shared Read

 Find Text Evidence

 Underline and read aloud the words *about* and *our*.

 Circle and read aloud the words with the long *a* sound spelled *ay*.

This is a tale about Frog and Snail. One **splendid** day, Snail sat in the grass. Just then, Frog hopped past.

mess Fissn

"Let's play!" said Snail.

"Yay!" said Frog. "Let's race to our school."

"Yes," said Snail. "To win, we must get inside the gate."

Shared Read

Ask any questions you may have about the text. Read to find the answer.

Underline and read aloud the words *animal, give,* and *carry.*

Snail was not a fast animal. He inched his way along the trail. Then Frog hopped past, fast, fast, fast!

"I will give you a tip," yelled Frog. "Hop like me. And don't carry that big shell!"

"I can't hop. I don't have long legs," said Snail. "And this shell is home."

Snail
crdlbb

🔍 **Find Text Evidence**

Ask any questions you may have about the text. Read to find the answer.

Talk about Frog. How did she get to the gate first?

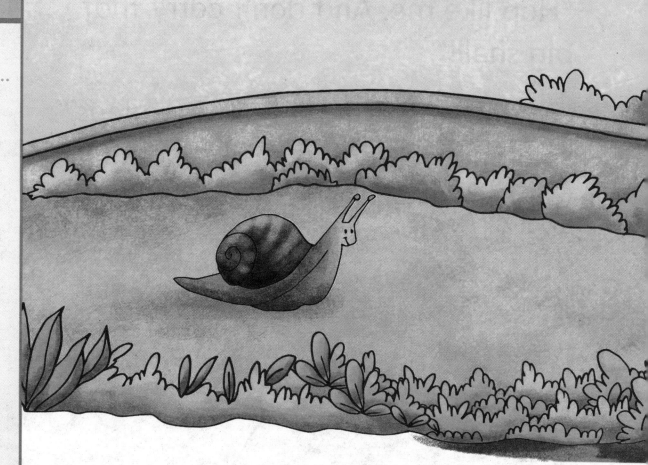

"I will win, then!" yelled Frog. "At this rate, it will take you eight days!"

Frog hopped past, fast, fast, fast! Snail inched along the trail.

Then Frog came to the gate.
"I made it," she bragged.
But the gate was locked!
Frog hopped up. But the gate
was too big.

Shared Read

 Find Text Evidence

Ask any other questions you have about the story. Then retell the story to find the answers.

Focus on Fluency

Take turns reading aloud to a partner.

- Read each word carefully.
- Read so it sounds like speech.

Frog sat and waited for Snail.
At last, Snail came.
"I can't get in!" wailed Frog.

Snail used his **special** sticky body
to slide past the gate.
"I win!" said Snail. Then he rested.
It had been a big day.

Vocabulary

 Listen to the sentences and look at the photos.

 Talk about the words.

 Write your own sentence using each word.

special

Penguins move in a **special** way.

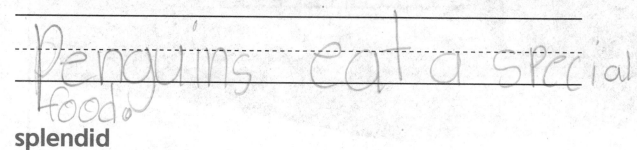

Penguins eat a special food.

splendid

A peacock has a **splendid** tail.

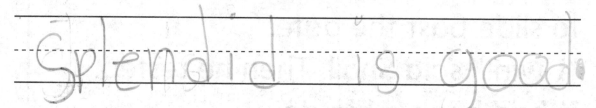

Splendid is good.

Use a Dictionary

If you don't know the meaning of a word, you can use a dictionary to learn its meaning.

Find Text Evidence

I'm not sure what *bragged* means. I will use a dictionary to look up *brag*, the base word of *bragged*. I learn that *brag* means "to talk about yourself in a proud manner."

> Then Frog came to the gate. "I made it," she bragged.

Your Turn

Use a dictionary to find the meaning of *wailed* on page 20. Write the meaning.

A **folktale** is a genre. A folktale is a story that has been told for many years. Folktales may have animal characters that act like humans.

 Reread to find out what makes this story a folktale.

 Share how you know it is a folktale.

Write two clues from the story that show it is a folktale.

Animal Character	How it Acts like a Human

Authors often give information in sequence, or the order of events. Think about what happens *first, next, then,* and *last* in the story to help you understand sequence.

 Reread "Snail and Frog Race."

 Use sequence words to talk about the events in the story.

Write about what happens *first, next, then* and *last.*

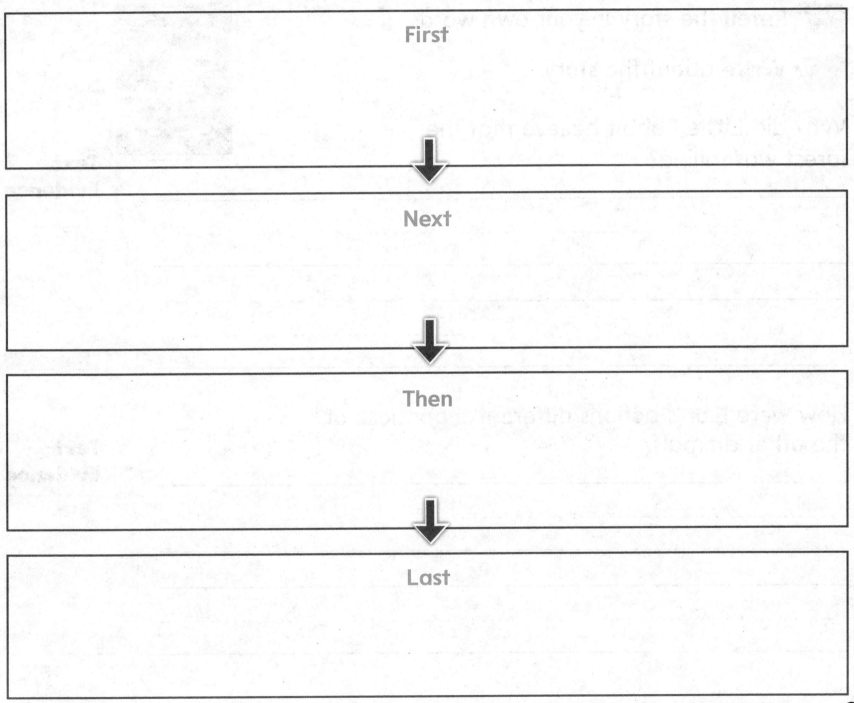

First

Next

Then

Last

Retell the story in your own words.

Write about the story.

Why did Little Rabbit believe that the
forest was falling?

Text Evidence

Page

_____

_____

_____

How were Lion's actions different than those of
the other animals?

Text Evidence

Page

_____

_____

_____

Connect to the **Anchor Text**

 Talk about how the stories are the same and different.

 Write about the stories.

Think about the ending of each story. What happens to both Little Rabbit and Frog?

_____

- -

_____

- -

_____

How do the animals in each of the stories use their bodies to help them?

_____

- -

_____

- -

_____

Make Inferences

Use details from the text to figure out things that aren't stated.

Little Rabbit learns. . . .

Frog learns . . .

Talk about the illustrations on pages 13 and 15. How is Little Rabbit feeling?

Write clues from the illustration that help you answer the question.

On page 13 Little Rabbit looks:	
On page 15 Little Rabbit looks:	

How do the illustrations help you know how Little Rabbit is feeling?

_____

- -

_____

- -

_____

Talk about what the animals are doing on pages 16–19.

 Write about what each animal does after it sees the other animals.

What does Deer do?	What do Ox and Tiger do?

How does the author show how the news about the forest spreads?

_____

- -

_____

- -

_____

Talk about the events on pages 24–27.
What does Lion do?

 Write clues that show how Lion is different
from the rest of the animals.

What the other animals do	What Lion does

How does the author change the story with Lion?

_____

- -

_____

_____

- -

_____

 **Write About It**

How do the animals
come to believe Little
Rabbit's story?

Animals Can Go Fast!

What moves at top speed? A plane? A train? How about a bird, a fish, or even a big cat? Many animals move fast. Mostly they are trying to catch other animals. Or trying not to get caught!

What helps them go fast? Let's look and learn.

 Read to find out about how fast some animals can move.

 Underline the sentences that tell you why animals move fast.

Talk about why the author chose this photo for the text.

Read the chart. It tells ways animals go fast to stay alive.

Animal	What Helps Them To Go Fast	Speed
Peregrine falcon	Wings, body shape	200 miles an hour
Cheetah	Long thin body, long legs, long tail	70 miles an hour
Sailfish	Foldable fin	68 miles an hour
Brown hare	Long hind legs	45 miles an hour

Underline the names of animals that have long legs.

Circle the text in the chart that tells how fast a cheetah can go.

Talk about what information the chart gives the reader.

Quick Tip

Read the headings in the chart first.

Talk about what you learn about these fast animals from the chart.

 Write clues from the chart.

What helps the peregrine falcon go fast?	
What helps the sailfish go fast?	

How does the author help you learn why each animal can move fast?

_____

- -

_____

- -

_____

Talk About It

How does the author show that these animals' bodies help them?

Animal Bodies

Step 1 Pick an animal to research. Find out how its body helps it live, move, or eat.

_____

- -

_____

Step 2 Decide what you want to know about the animal. Write your questions.

_____

- -

_____

- -

_____

_____

Step 3 Decide where to find the information you need.

Step 4 Write what you learned about the animal.

_____

- -

_____

- -

_____

- -

_____

- -

_____

- -

_____

- -

_____

Step 5 Draw the animal. Label its body parts.

Step 6 Choose how to present your work.

Talk about what the caption tells you about hares.

 Compare what these hares and the animals in "Animals Can Go Fast!" do to stay alive. Use complete sentences.

Quick Tip

You can compare the animals using these sentence starters:

Hares have . . .

Animals that move fast have . . .

The arctic hare's fur turns white in winter. This makes the hare hard to find in the snow.

image courtesy National Gallery of Art

What I Know Now

Think about the texts you heard and read this week about animals and their bodies. Write what you learned.

_____

_____

_____

_____

 Think about other animals you want to learn about. Tell your partner.

 Share one thing you learned this week about folktales.

Essential Question How do animals help each other?

Talk about how the bird and the hippo help each other.

 Write what you know about these two animals.

Hippo	Bird
pretets help get food a ride	eats pets skrach

Shared Read

Find Text Evidence

Read the title. Look at the photo. Think about what you want to learn from this text.

Circle and read aloud the word with the long *e* sound spelled *ea*.

Essential Question

? How do animals help each other?

A Team of Fish

Nonfiction

real.

Fiction

Shared Read

Find Text Evidence

Underline and read aloud the words *blue, into,* and *or.*

Ask any questions you may have about the text. Read to find the answer.

Fish swim in lakes and creeks. Fish swim in deep blue seas or oceans.

Let's dive into the water. Let's look at fish!

Fish can swim alone. Fish can swim with a **partner**.

Fish can swim in a bunch, too. A bunch of fish is called a school.

Shared Read

A school has lots of fish. They are a team.

The fish help each other. They look for food together.

Reinhard Dirscherl/Alamy

Fish eat lots of things. Some fish eat small animals. Some fish eat other fish!

These catfish eat together for safety.

Shared Read

Georgette Douwma/Photographer's Choice/Getty Images

 Find Text Evidence

 Circle and read aloud the word with the long *e* sound spelled *ie*.

Ask any questions you may have about the text. Read to find the answer.

It can be unsafe to swim alone. What is the chief reason? **Danger!** A fish can get snapped up!

But a fish can hide in a school.

Fish in a school have a neat trick. The fish swim close together.

Big fish will not mess with them because they look like one huge fish.

These crescent-tail bigeye fish swim in a school to fool big fish.

Shared Read

Find Text Evidence

Retell the text using the photos and words.

Focus on Fluency

Take turns reading aloud to a partner.

- Read each word carefully.

- Read so it sounds like speech.

This big fish wants to eat. But it stays away. The school looks like a huge fish that may eat him!

Fish in a school keep each other safe.

A school is a good place for a fish to be!

Hundreds of barracuda fish swim in a school together.

Vocabulary

 Listen to the sentences and look at the photos.

 Talk about the words.

 Write your own sentence using each word.

danger

Mom keeps her cub out of **danger**.

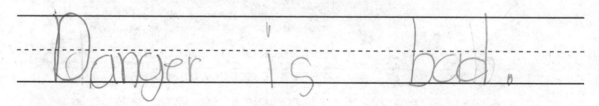
Danger is bad.

partner

A **partner** is a big help.

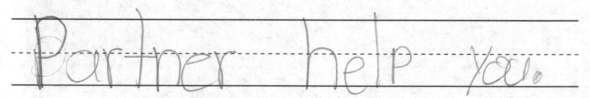
Partner help you.

If you don't know what a word means, look at other words in the sentence for clues.

Find Text Evidence

I'm not sure what *oceans* means. The words *swim in deep blue seas* give me hints about the meaning. I think *oceans* are some kind of water.

Fish swim in lakes and creeks. Fish swim in deep blue seas or oceans.

Your Turn

What words can help you figure out the meaning of *school* on page 45?

_____

- - - - - - - - - - - - - - - - - - -

_____

- - - - - - - - - - - - - - - - - - -

_____

- - - - - - - - - - - - - - - - - - -

_____

Martin Strmiska/Alamy

Nonfiction is a genre. A nonfiction text can give facts about real things. It can be organized by description.

 Reread "A Team of Fish" to find out how the text is organized.

 Share what the author is describing on page 44.

Write about what the author describes on page 45 and page 47.

A Team of Fish	What It Describes
Page 44	
Page 45	
Page 47	

The main idea is what the text is mostly about.
Key details give information about the main
idea.

 Reread "A Team of Fish."

 Talk about the main idea and key details in
the text. Use the words and pictures.

Write the main idea and key details
about why fish swim in schools.

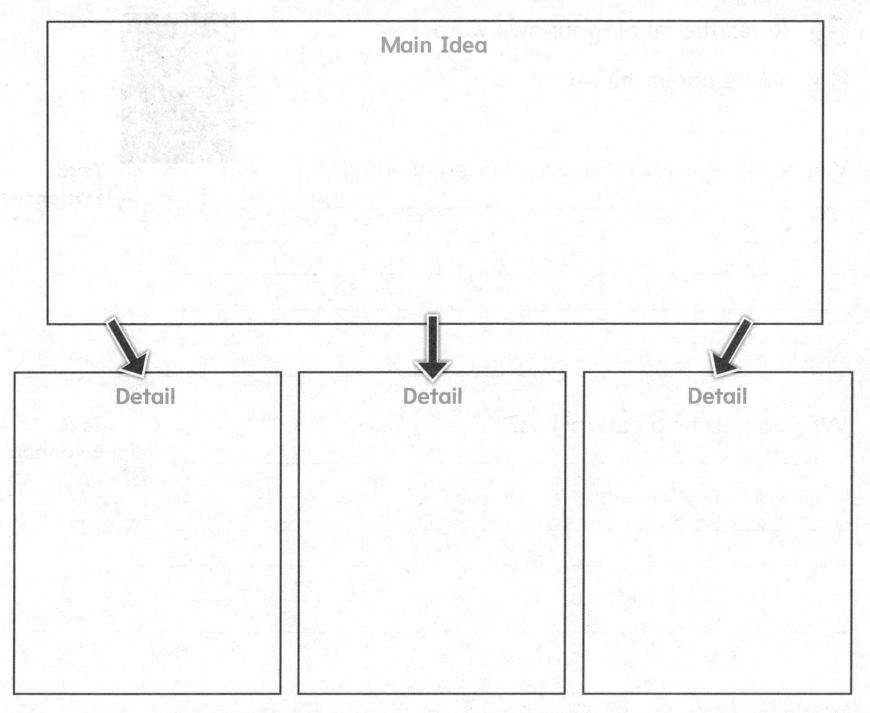

Main Idea

Detail

Detail

Detail

Retell the text in your own words.

Write about the text.

Why does the clown fish live in a sea anemone?

_____

_____

_____

_____

Text Evidence

Page

Why do ants help caterpillars?

_____

_____

_____

_____

Text Evidence

Page

Talk about how the texts are the same and different.

 Write about the texts.

How are the texts alike?

_____

- -

_____

- -

_____

Why is it important for animals to help each other?

_____

- -

_____

- -

Focus on Fluency

Take turns reading aloud to a partner from *Animal Teams*.

- Read each word correctly.

- Read so it sounds like speech.

- Pause after each period.

Talk about how the animals on pages 42–43 help each other.

Write clues from the text and photos to complete the chart.

What Text Says	What Photos Show

How do the text and photos help you understand how the animals work as a team?

_____

- -

_____

- -

_____

Talk about the question the author asks at the end of page 44.

 Write clues from the text that answer the author's question.

Answer

How does the author help you understand the information about this animal team?

_____

- -

_____

- -

_____

Share how the animals on pages 48–51 help each other.

Write what you learn about animal teams on these pages.

Pages 48–49	Pages 50–51

Why does the author show so many different animal teams?

_____

- -

_____

- -

_____

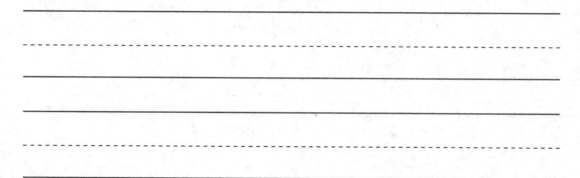

Write About It

Which animal team do you think is the most interesting? Why? Write your answer in your writer's notebook.

"Busy as a Bee"

Lots of worker bees help make honey. They help keep the hive clean, too.

Worker bees make wax cups called honeycombs.

Read to find out how bees work together as a team.

Circle the word that tells what wax cups are called.

Talk about how the author shows that bees are busy.

(t)Jan Rietz/Nordic Photos/Getty Images; (b)Ted Horowitz/Corbis/Getty Images

Every hive has a queen bee. She lays all the eggs.

A hive has drone bees, too. A drone's job is to help the queen make eggs.

A queen bee is with her drones in the hive.

Underline the sentence that tells what a queen bee does.

Circle the text that tells who else lives in the hive.

Talk about the photo and the caption. Why does the author include both?

Quick Tip

Think about what the photo and caption tell you about bees.

Talk about the title of the text.

Write clues about what each bee does.

Worker Bees	Queen Bee	Drone Bees

How does the title help you understand
the main idea of the text?

_____

- -

_____

- -

_____

Talk About It

How does the author
show that every bee
in a hive has a special
job?

Animal Teams

Step 1 **Pick** a team of animals to research.

_____

- -

_____

Step 2 **Decide** where to find the information you need.

_____

- -

_____

Step 3 **Draw** the animal team you learned about. Use labels to name each animal.

Step 4 **Write** what you learned about the animal team.

_____

- -

_____

- -

_____

_____

- -

_____

_____

- -

_____

Step 5 **Choose** how to present your work.

Make Connections

 Talk about how the birds in the photo are a team.

 Compare how these birds are similar to the school of fish you read about.

Quick Tip

You can talk about this photo using these sentence starters:

Birds fly together to . . .

The birds help one another . . .

kevin palmer photography/Moment Open/Getty Images

It is safe to be in a big group.
These birds flock together to stay safe.

What I Know Now

Think about the texts you heard and read
this week about how animals help each other.
Write what you learned.

_____

- -

_____

_____

- -

_____

- -

_____

 Think about other animals teams you
want to learn about. Tell your partner.

 Share one thing you learned this week
about nonfiction.

Talk About It

Essential Question **How do animals survive in nature?**

Talk about how this eagle gets its food. How does it use its body? Be sure to speak clearly.

Write about how eagles hunt for food.

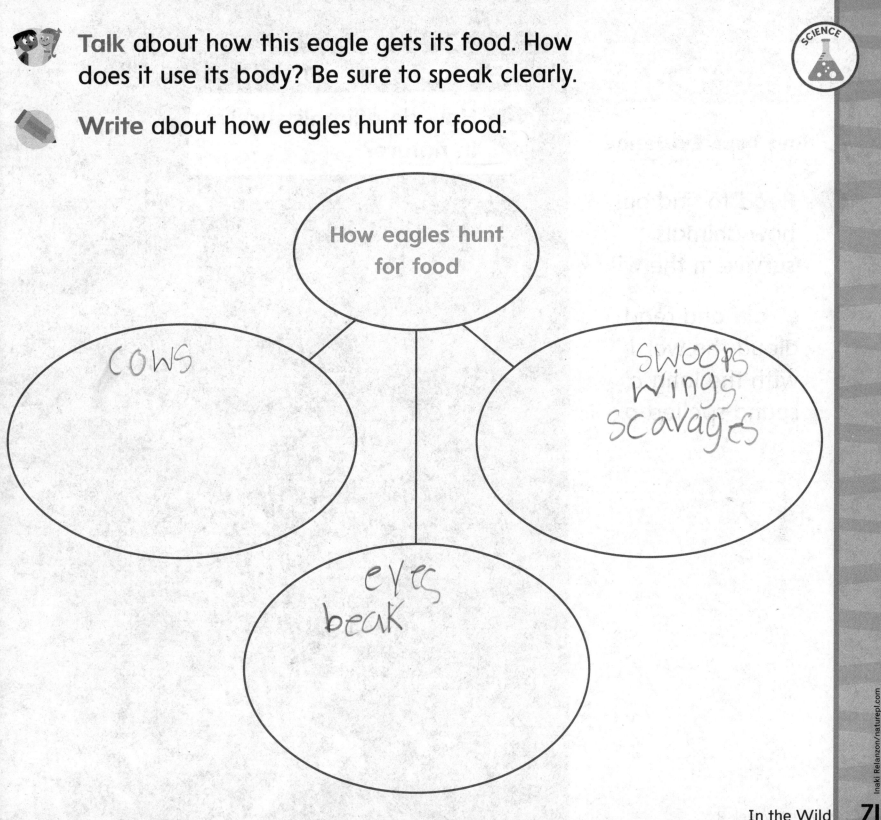

How eagles hunt for food

cows

swoops wings scavages

eyes beak

Shared Read

 Find Text Evidence

 Read to find out how animals survive in the wild.

Circle and read aloud the word with the long *o* sound spelled *o*.

Essential Question

? How do animals survive in nature?

GO WILD!

Shared Read

 Find Text Evidence

Underline and read aloud the words *food, more,* and *find.*

Ask yourself any questions you may have about the text. Read to find the answer.

Animals need food to live and grow. But all animals don't eat the same things. Some big animals such as hippos eat plants. A hippo can eat more than 130 pounds of grass!

Some small animals eat plants, too. A squirrel eats loads of plant seeds. They like nuts and grains. A squirrel can smell a nut and find it even in the snow!

Shared Read

 Find Text Evidence

 Talk about the big cat. How does it hunt?

Circle and read aloud the words with the long *o* sound spelled *oa*.

Some animals hunt and eat other animals. First this big cat runs fast to catch its meal. Then it will use its claws and teeth to eat.

Andy Rouse/The Image Bank/Getty Images

catch

Frogs and toads **seek** insects and snails to eat. A big frog goes after mice, too. But frogs and toads have no teeth. So they must gulp down their meal!

craftvision/Vetta/Getty Images

Ask yourself any questions you may have about the text. Read to find the answer.

Underline and read aloud the words *over* and *warm*.

Some animals eat both plants and animals. An ostrich eats seeds and leaves. But it will **search** all over for insects, snakes, and lizards as well.

Carl & Ann Purcell/Corbis Documentary/Getty Images

hIbeR NAte

A painted turtle eats plants, fish, and frogs. This reptile lives in lakes and ponds. It likes the cold water at first. But then it will come up on land to get warm.

Find Text Evidence

Retell the text using the photos and words.

Focus on Fluency

Take turns reading aloud to a partner.

- Read each word carefully.

- Read so it sounds like speech.

A bear may start its day by eating plants. Next, it may go fishing in a lake. After that, a bear may go hunting. Then, it may even go to a campsite.

Andy Rouse/The Image Bank/Getty Images

Most bears will eat plants, animals, and people food. Is there any food left here to eat? If so, a bear will find it! In the wild, animals find food in lots of places.

Vocabulary

Listen to the sentences and look at the photos.

Talk about the words.

Write your own sentence using each word.

search

Do bees **search** for plants?

I search for a be
aty.

seek

A bear will **seek** out ripe berries.

I like to play
hide and seek.

Word Categories

As we read, we can look for groups of words that are alike in some ways.

Find Text Evidence

I can find words that fit in the same category. The words *seeds, nuts,* and *grains* name things that squirrels eat. I will look for other words that fit in the category of *things that animals eat.*

Frogs and toads seek (insects) and (snails) to eat. A big frog goes after (mice) too.

Your Turn

What words belong in the same category as *animal names* on page 78?

_____

_____

_____

_____

_____

craftvision/Vetta/Getty Images

Nonfiction is a genre. A nonfiction text can give facts about real things. It can be organized by description.

Reread "Go Wild!" to find out how this text is organized.

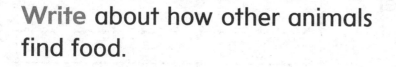
Share what squirrels eat. How does the author describe how they find food?

Write about how other animals find food.

Animal	Description of How It Finds Food
1.	1.
2.	2.
3.	3.

Remember, the **main idea** is what the text is mostly about. **Key details** give information about the main idea.

 Reread "Go Wild!"

 Talk about the key detail about squirrels on page 75. Write it on the chart.

 Write more key details from the text. Then think about what the key details have in common to write the main idea.

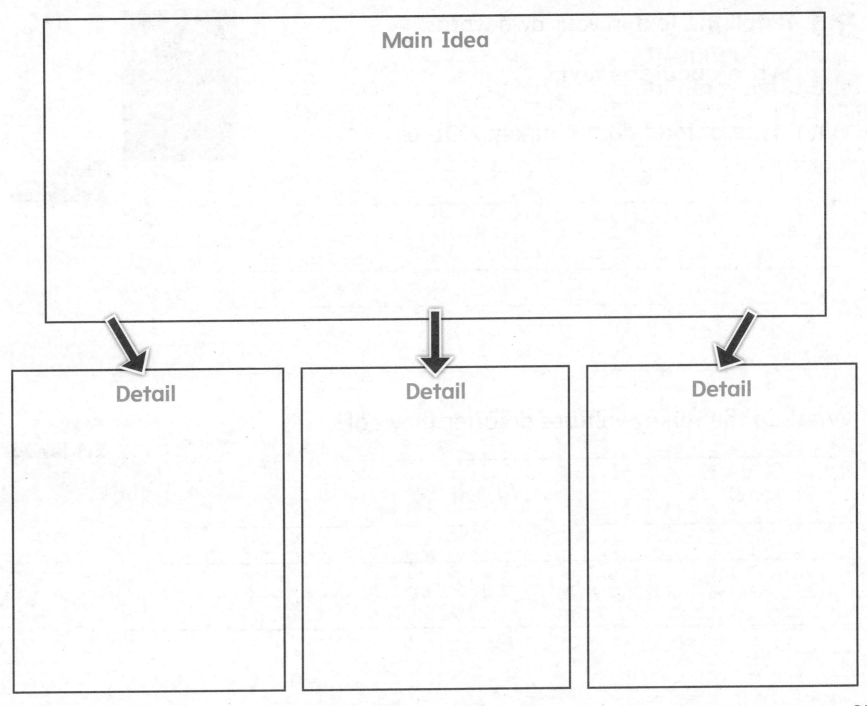

Main Idea

Detail

Detail

Detail

Retell the text in your own words.

Write about the text.

What type of food do the turkey vultures look for?

Text Evidence

Pages

_____

- - - - - - - - - - - - - - - - -

_____

- - - - - - - - - - - - - - - - -

_____

What do the turkey vultures do after they eat?

Text Evidence

Page

_____

- - - - - - - - - - - - - - - - -

_____

- - - - - - - - - - - - - - - - -

_____

Talk about how the texts are the same and different.

Write about the texts.

How are the texts alike?

_____

- -

_____

- -

_____

How are vultures different than most animals?

_____

- -

_____

_____

- -

_____

Make Inferences

Use details to figure out things that are not stated.

What do the authors of each text describe?

Talk about what the vultures are doing on pages 64–67.

Write clues from the text to complete the chart. Use the illustrations to help you.

What does the text describe?	
What do the illustrations show?	

How does the author help you picture what is happening?

_____

- -

_____

- -

_____

Talk about the illustrations on pages 76–79.

Write clues from the illustrations that help you understand what the vultures are doing.

Pages 76–77	Pages 78–79

How do the illustrations help you understand how vultures eat?

_____

- -

_____

- -

_____

Talk about how the author describes the vultures' wings on pages 82 and 86.

 Write the words on the chart.

Page 82	Page 86

What do the author's words help you picture?
Share your answer.

_____

- -

_____

- -

_____

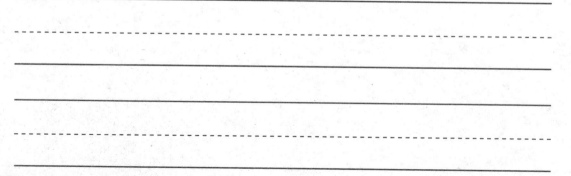
Write About It

How do vultures use their body parts to help them find food?

"When It's Snowing"

 Talk about the illustration on pages 90–91.

 Write clues that show how it feels outside and inside the mouse's house.

Outside	Inside

How does the illustration help you understand the poem's setting?

_____

_____

_____

Talk about the beat you hear in the poem.
Clap the rhythm you hear in lines 1 and 2.

Write the number of beats that you hear.

Number of beats in lines 1 and 2	
Number of beats in lines 3 and 4	

How does the rhythm of the poem make you feel?

_____

- -

_____

_____

- -

_____

Quick Tip

You can clap your hands as you read a poem to find the beat.

Talk about the question in the first paragraph.

Write clues that help you know how the poet feels about the mouse.

How poet refers to the mouse	What poet asks mouse

How do you know the poet cares about the mouse?

_____

- - - - - - - - - - - - - - - - - - -

_____

_____

- - - - - - - - - - - - - - - - - - -

_____

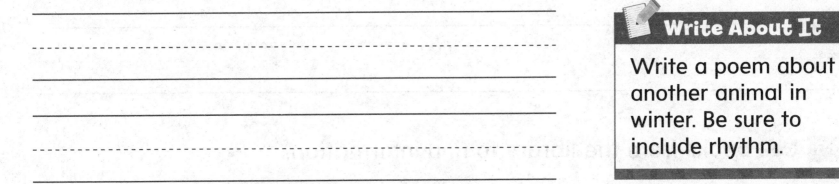

Write About It

Write a poem about another animal in winter. Be sure to include rhythm.

Animal Life Cycle

Step 1 **Pick** an animal to research.
Find out about its life cycle.

_____

- -

_____

Step 2 **Decide** what you want to know about
the animal. Write your questions.

_____

- -

_____

_____

- -

_____

_____

- -

_____

Step 3 **Use** books from the library to find information.

Step 4 Write what you learned about the animal.

_____

- -

_____

- -

_____

- -

_____

- -

_____

- -

_____

- -

_____

Step 5 Draw the animal.

Step 6 Choose how to present your work.

Talk about what the orca in the photo is doing.

 Compare how the food orcas eat is different to what vultures eat.

Quick Tip

You can compare using these sentence starters:

Vultures eat . . .

Orcas eat . . .

Tory Kallman/Moment/Getty Images

Orcas eat live fish and animals. They hunt for food in the sea.

What I Know Now

Think about the texts you heard and read this week about how animals survive in the wild. Write what you learned.

_____

- -

_____

- -

_____

- -

_____

 Think about other animals you want to learn about. Tell your partner.

 Share one thing you learned this week about nonfiction.

Essential Question What insects do you know? How are they alike and different?

Talk about this caterpillar. How is it like other bugs that you know?

Write what you know about caterpillars.

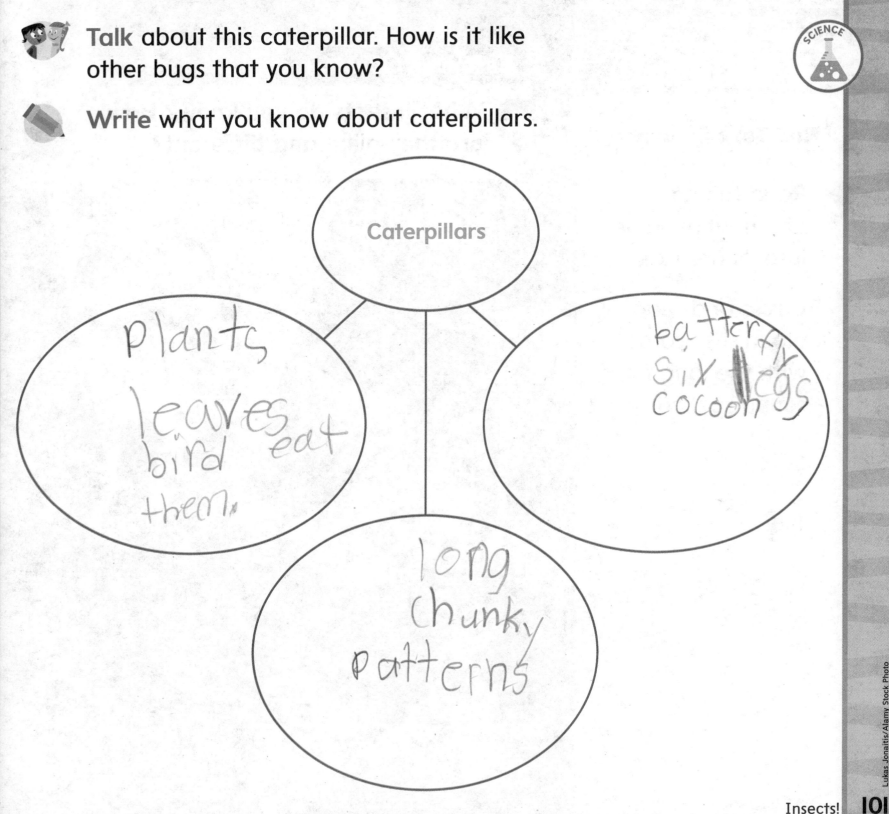

Caterpillars

plants, leaves eat bird them.

batterfly six legs cocoon eggs

long chunky patterns

Shared Read

 Find Text Evidence

 Read to find out about what some insects are like.

Circle and read aloud the word with the long *i* sound spelled *-y*.

Essential Question

 What insects do you know? How are they alike and different?

Creep Low, Fly High

Shared Read

 Underline and read aloud the words *laugh* and *listen*.

Think about the words *zip around*. How do they help you picture how Ladybug moves?

Bug Boasts

The Sun came up over a big field. Five bug pals met to chat and laugh.

Grasshopper boasted a bit. "I can hop to the top of any plant!"

"Well, I can dash fast," bragged Ant.

"Listen!" hummed Bee. "I can buzz as I fly high."

"And I can zip around on **fancy** spotted wings!" smiled Ladybug.

Find Text Evidence

Think about how Caterpillar feels. Why does he sigh and creep away?

Circle and read aloud the word with the long *i* sound spelled *-igh*.

"Not I," sighed Caterpillar. "I just creep, creep, creep." Then he crept away.

"Come back!" his pals wailed. But Caterpillar did not.

Missing!

It was time for lunch. The bugs did not see Caterpillar. He was missing! Where did he go?

Find Text Evidence

Talk about what Bee says. Picture the bird in your mind. What do you think it was doing?

Underline the words *know*, *where*, *flew* and *caught*.

"I think I know where he is!" cried Ant. "He is hiding because he feels bad."

"I think that's right," nodded Grasshopper. "Let's find him. We can cheer him up!"

The two rushed away.

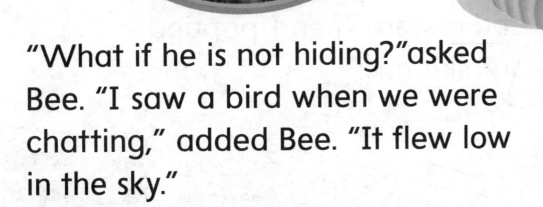

"What if he is not hiding?"asked
Bee. "I saw a bird when we were
chatting," added Bee. "It flew low
in the sky."

"What if it caught our pal?" cried
Ladybug. "We must find out!
Maybe we can save him!"

The two flew away.

Still a Pal

The bugs did not find Caterpillar. Many days went by. The pals were sad. Then one day they saw a **beautiful** bug with gold wings.

"Hi! I'm back!" the bug called as he flew by. "I wrapped up and rested. Then I popped out like this!"

"It's me—Butterfly! I used to be Caterpillar!" cried Butterfly.

"But you are not the same," sighed Ant.

"But I am still a pal," said Butterfly. "And now I can flit and dip! Let's go have some fun!"

Vocabulary

 Listen to the sentences and look at the photos.

 Talk about the words.

 Write your own sentence using each word.

beautiful

The butterfly has **beautiful** wings.

My mom is beautiful

fancy

We are wearing **fancy** hats.

My house is fancy.

John Foxx/Stockbyte/Getty Images; LWA/Dann Tardif/Blend Images/Getty Images

When you are not sure of what a word means, you can look at how it is used in the sentence.

Find Text Evidence

I'm not sure what *chat* means. The word *laugh* is a hint. I know that the bugs are pals so they must have been talking together. I think *chat* means *to talk in a friendly way.*

Five bug pals met to chat and laugh.

Your Turn

What is the meaning of *dash* on page 105 of the story?

_____

- - - - - - - - - - - - - - -

_____

- - - - - - - - - - - - - - -

_____

- - - - - - - - - - - - - - -

_____

A fantasy story can have characters that could not exist in real life. It often has a problem and solution.

Creep Low, Fly High

 Reread to find out what the problem and solution are in this fantasy story.

 Share how you know the characters could not exist in real life.

Write about Caterpillar's problems. How does he solve them?

What is the problem?	What is the solution?
1.	1.
2.	2.
3.	3.

Point of view is the way that a character in the story thinks or feels.

Creep Low, Fly High

 Reread "Creep Low, Fly High."

 Talk about each character's point of view in the story.

Write about how each character feels.

Character	Clue	Point of View

Retell the story in your own words.

Write about the story.

How does the boy catch the fly?

_____

- -

_____

- -

_____

Text Evidence

Page

What convinces the judges that
Fly Guy is a pet?

_____

- -

_____

- -

Text Evidence

Page

Talk about how the stories are the same and different. Use complete sentences.

Write about the stories.

How are the stories alike?

_____
- -
_____
- -
_____

How do the insects in each story move about?

_____
- -
_____
_____
- -
_____

Quick Tip

Use clues in the stories to figure out how the insects move.

Fly Guy shows he can . . .

Ladybug says she can . . .

Talk about how the fly and the boy are feeling on pages 102–103.

 Write clues from the pictures and text that show you how the characters are feeling.

How the Fly Feels	How the Boy Feels

How does the author show you how the fly and the boy feel?

_____

- -

_____

- -

_____

Talk about the events on pages 112–115.
How do the judges' faces change?

 Write clues from the illustrations that
help you understand how the judges feel.

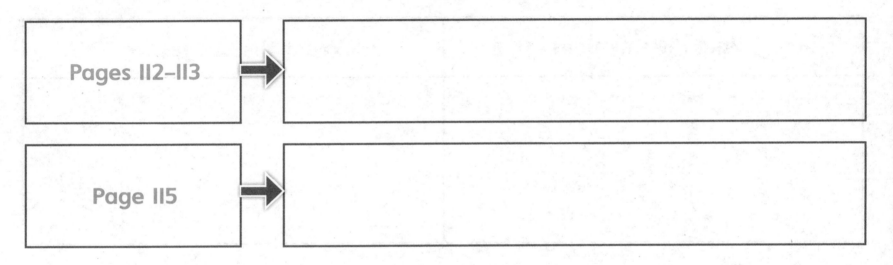

Pages 112–113	

Page 115	

How do the illustrations help you know
the judges' point of view?

_____

- -

_____

- -

_____

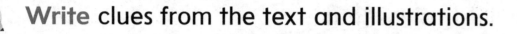 

Talk about pages 117–121. How does
Fly Guy show the judges that he is a pet?

Write clues from the text and illustrations.

What Fly Guy Does	What the Judges Do

How does the author show that Fly Guy
can be a pet?

_____

- -

_____

- -

_____

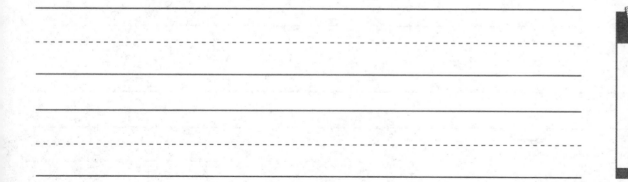

Write About It

Why do Buzz's parents
and the judges change
their minds about
Fly Guy?

"Meet the Insects"

The Body of an Insect

All insects have six legs and three body parts. Insects have no bones. The outside of an insect's body is hard. It protects the insect's body. Most insects have antennae and wings.

Read to find out what insects can do.

Underline the clue that tells you what most insects have.

Talk about the heading. How does the heading help you understand the text on this page?

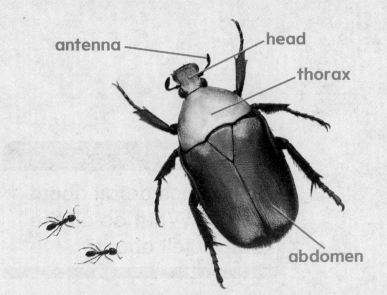

antenna — head

thorax

abdomen

Brian Hagiwara/Stockbyte/Getty Images

Insect Senses

Insects use their senses to find food. A fly smells with its antennae.
It tastes with its feet. That's why flies like to land on food.

Insects do not see the same as we do. Many insects have more than two eyes. A grasshopper has five!

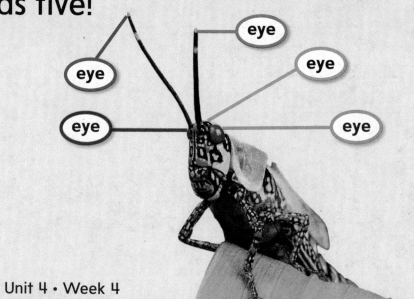

Simon Murrell/Cultura/Getty Images

 Circle the text that tells what a fly does with its feet.

 Underline the sentence that tells how many eyes a grasshopper has.

Talk about how the author uses headings to organize the text.

Quick Tip

Read each detail about the fly. What do all the details tell about?

Talk about what the photos help you understand about insects.

 Write clues from the photos to complete the chart.

What information does the photo on page 123 provide?	
What information does the photo on page 124 provide?	

How do the labels help you understand what insects are like?

_____

_____

_____

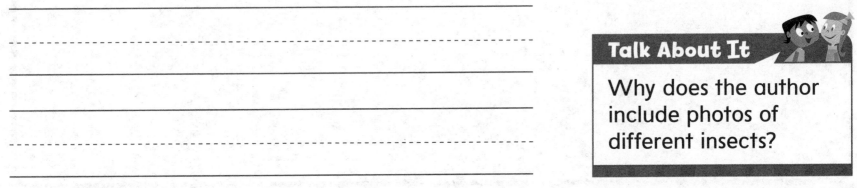

Talk About It

Why does the author include photos of different insects?

Two Bugs

Step 1 Pick two insects you read about to compare their body parts.

_____

- -

_____

Step 2 Use books from the library or the Internet to find the information you need.

Step 3 Draw the insects below.

Step 4 Write about how the insects are alike and different.

_____
- -
_____

_____
- -
_____

_____
- -
_____

_____
- -
_____

Step 5 Choose how to present your work.

Talk about what the photo shows you about dragonflies.

 Compare how the body parts of this dragonfly are alike or different from other insects you read about.

> ### Quick Tip
>
> You can describe dragonflies using these sentence starters:
>
> *Dragonflies have . . .*
>
> *Dragonflies are insects because . . .*

A dragonfly has three body parts. This dragonfly has a blue head and abdomen. Its thorax is green with black stripes.

ChatchawalPhumkaew/iStock/Getty Images

What I Know Now

Think about the texts you heard and read this week about how insects are alike and different. Write what you learned.

_____

- -

_____

- -

_____

- -

_____

 Think about other insects you want to learn about. Tell your partner.

 Share one thing you learned this week about fantasy.

Talk About It

Talk about this trainer. What do you think she is teaching this dog?

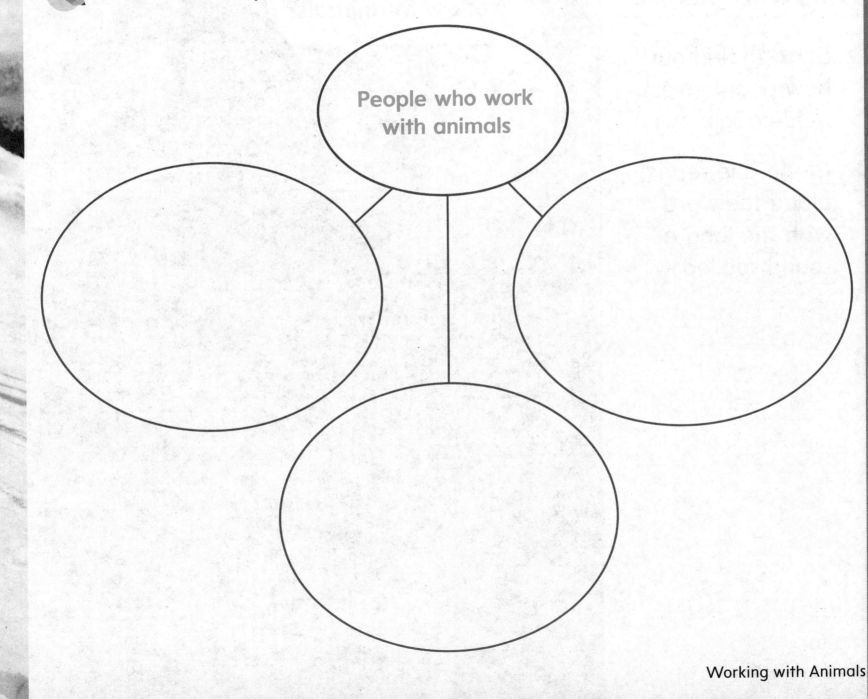 **Write** about people who work with animals.

People who work
with animals

Shared Read

Find Text Evidence

 Read to find out how people train guide dogs.

Circle and read aloud the word with the long *e* sound spelled *-y*.

Essential Question

? How do people work with animals?

From Puppy to Guide Dog

TIME FOR KIDS®

Most dogs are pets. But some dogs help people. What is the key to making a dog a good helping dog?

Underline and read aloud the word *found*.

Picture in your mind a lazy or fussy dog. Why do you think it could not be a good guide dog?

A Buddy-to-Be

Mickey is a cute and **clever** puppy. He runs, jumps, and plays. One day, when he grows up a bit, Mickey will be a helping dog. He will be a daily buddy to a person who cannot see.

Helping dogs are called guide dogs. To be a guide dog, a puppy must be bright. It cannot be lazy or fussy. The puppy will need to learn many skills. A new home is found for the puppy when it is eight weeks old.

▼ Guide dogs can be big or tiny.

Fact

Most guide dogs are Labrador retrievers. They are very intelligent and easy to train.

Ryan McVay/Photolibrary

Find Text Evidence

 Talk about how a family can help train a puppy. What can they do?

Circle and read aloud the word with the long *e* sound spelled *-ey*.

A Family of Trainers

A puppy like Mickey stays with a family for at least one year. The family plays with it and feeds it. They help the puppy stay healthy and teach the puppy a lot.

▲ Each puppy has checkups at the vet.

Fact

10,000 people in the U.S. and Canada use guide dogs.

Jim Craigmyle/Corbis/Getty Images

Each puppy learns how to act nicely with people and with other animals. The family gets the dog used to a lot of tasks and settings. Puppies may visit many kinds of places in the city. They go to homes and shops.

▲ This dog watches its favorite team.

▼ Every dog must be trained by itself.

Shared Read

 Find Text Evidence

Picture a dog that stays right near its trainer. Why do you think it is important for the dog to do this?

 Underline and read aloud the words *near, woman,* and *hard.*

Learning New Tasks

As time goes by, the dogs are trained how to go across the street. The dog stays right near the trainer. It learns to stop at a red **signal**. This will help the dog safely lead a person who cannot see the traffic.

 Fact

Guide dogs are allowed in restaurants, stores, school—any place a person can go.

 This guide dog learns to cross a street.

Some guide dogs can be trained to help a man or a woman who cannot move or walk. He or she might need help with a lot of hard tasks both inside and outside the home.

A dog can be trained to get an elevator and to reach objects.

Retell the text using the photos and words from the text.

Focus on Fluency

Take turns reading aloud to a partner.

- Read each word carefully.
- Read so it sounds like speech.

Yan Sheng/CNImaging/Newscom

Eyes and Ears

Some dogs are trained to help people who cannot hear. If the dog hears a bell ringing or a yell, it would lightly tug or poke the person with its nose.

▼ A dog can be taught to alert its owner to sounds.

Fact

Guide dogs should not be bothered while working.

Ready to Guide

Training a puppy for a year is not an easy job. Owners may call or write to thank the family that raised their puppy.

Training a guide dog helps a lot of people!

Vocabulary

 Listen to the sentences and look at the photos.

 Talk about the words.

 Write your own sentence using each word.

clever

This bird is very **clever**.

_____

- -

_____

signal

The trainer gives a **signal**.

_____

- -

_____

If you don't know what a word means, you can look at its root word to figure out the meaning.

Find Text Evidence

I'm not sure what *helping* means. The word *help* is a hint. I know it means "to give or do something needed or useful." I can figure out that *helping* means "doing something needed or useful."

Mickey will be a helping dog.

Your Turn

What is the meaning of the word *training* on page 141?

_____

_____

_____

_____

_____

_____

_____

Juniors Bildarchiv GmbH/age fotostock

A **nonfiction** text can tell facts about real things. It can use photos to give information. Captions give more information about photos.

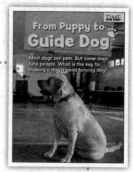

 Reread to find out how this text uses photos and captions.

 Share what you learn from the photo and the blue caption under the photo on page 136.

 Write what you learn from the photos and blue captions on pages 138 and 140.

This nonfiction text tells about

The photo and caption on page 138 tell me

The photo and caption on page 140 tell me

Sequence **is the way that an author presents information in time order. Think about what happens** *first, next, then,* **and** *last* **in the text to help you understand sequence.**

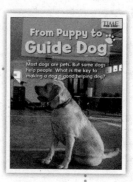

  Reread "From Puppy to Guide Dog."

Talk about the sequence of what happens to a guide dog puppy.

Write the order of steps needed to train a guide dog puppy.

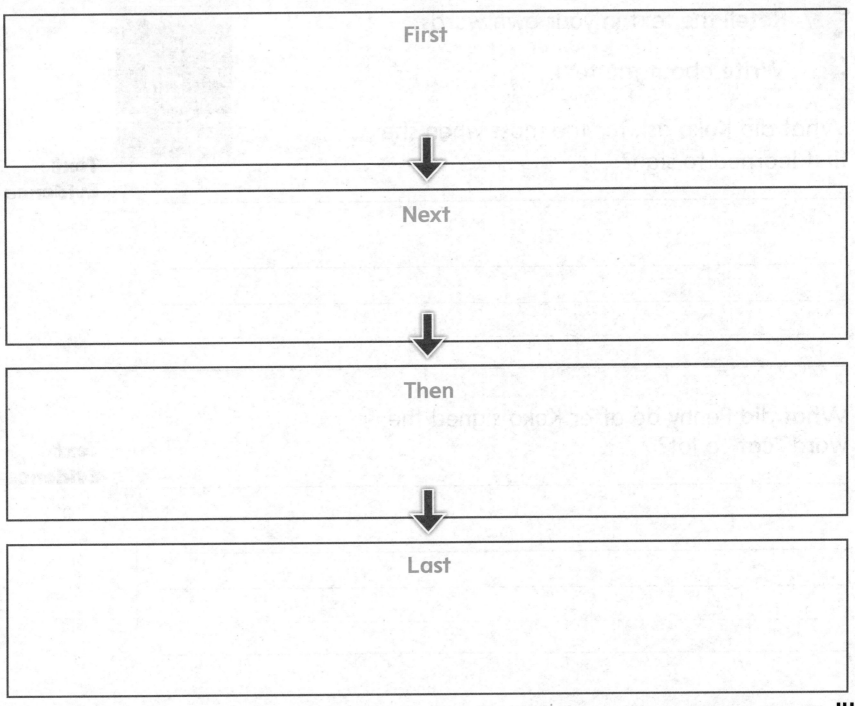

First

Next

Then

Last

Retell the text in your own words.

Write about the text.

What did Koko ask for the most when she first learned to sign?

Text Evidence

Page

What did Penny do after Koko signed the word "cat" a lot?

Text Evidence

Page

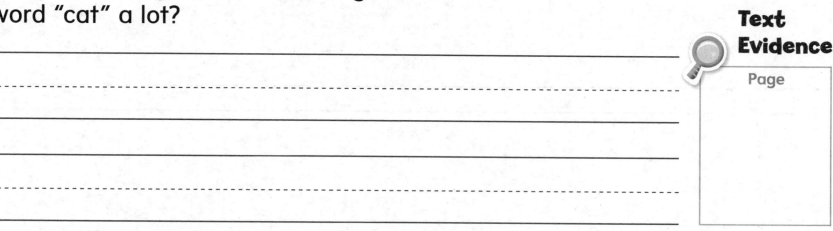

Talk about how the texts are the same and different.

Write about the text.

What is similar about guide dogs and an animal like Koko?

_____

_____

_____

Think about what guide dogs and vets, like Penny, do. Tell why they are important jobs.

_____

_____

_____

_____

Combine Information

As you read each text, think about how your ideas about Koko change.

Working with Animals **149**

Talk about the first thing Penny taught Koko.

Write clues from the text to complete the chart.

What does Penny teach Koko first?	What does Penny teach Koko next?

Why does the author present information in order?

_____

- -

_____

- -

_____

Talk about the signs Koko makes on pages 132–133.

Write what the captions tell you.

Page 132	Page 133

How do the captions help you understand the photos?

_____

- -

_____

_____

- -

_____

Write About It

What benefits did Koko gain by learning sign language?

Save Our Bees!

Bees need our help!
Many bees are dying.
Scientists think that bugs
or diseases are hurting bees.
Bees are important to us.

Beekeepers work with bees.

©Monty Rakusen/cultura/Corbis

 Read to find out how you can help save bees.

 Circle the word in the caption that tells who works with bees.

 Talk about why the author included exclamation marks. What does this tell you?

You can help bees by planting flowers. Bees eat nectar from flowers. You can build a bee nest. Bees can build nests in a bee block. Together we can help save bees!

This is a bee block. You can make it out of wood.

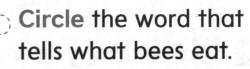 **Underline** the word in the caption that tells what you can use to make a bee block.

 Circle the word that tells what bees eat.

 Talk about what the author is able to explain by including captions.

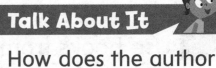

Talk About It

How does the author show that bees can still be saved?

Caring for Animals

Step 1 **Pick** one of the following two jobs to research:

veterinarian   zookeeper

Step 2 **Decide** what you want to know about this job. Write your questions.

_____
- -
_____
_____
- -
_____
_____
- -
_____

Step 3 **Use** books from the library to find the information you need.

Step 4 Write what you learned about the job you researched.

_____

- -

_____

- -

_____

- -

_____

- -

_____

- -

_____

Step 5 Draw something you learned.

Step 6 Choose how to present your work.

Talk about how people worked with pigeons.

 Compare how the way people worked with pigeons is similar to how people work with guide dogs.

Quick Tip

You can describe how people worked with pigeons using these sentence starters:

A person attached . . .

The pigeon would . . .

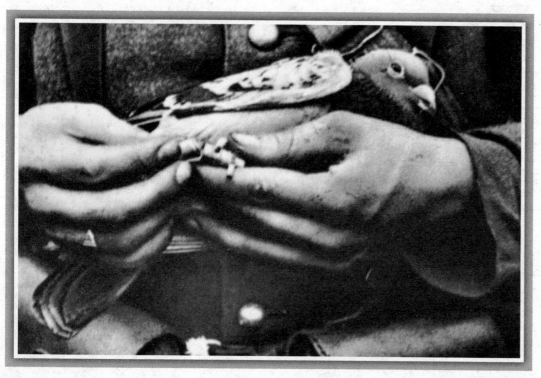

World History Archive/Alamy

Long ago, pigeons carried important messages that were tied to their legs. They would fly and take the messages to people far away.

What I Know Now

Think about the texts you heard and read this week about how people work with animals. Write what you learned.

_____

- -

_____

- -

_____

- -

_____

 Think about what else you would like to learn about working with animals.

 Share one thing you learned this week about nonfiction.

Writing and Grammar

Steve

I wrote a poem about my favorite animal. My poem has rhythm and words that rhyme.

Poem

My poem has rhythm. The words and syllables make a beat.

Student Model

Go, Tiger, Go!

I am a wild tiger,

I'm big and I'm strong,

My claws are sharp,

My tail is long!

Poem

My poem also has
words that rhyme.
They have the same
ending sounds.

I sleep in the day,

I hunt in the night,

Soon I will eat,

It's time for a bite!

 Talk about what
makes Steve's writing
a poem.

 Ask any questions you
have about the poem.

Circle the words
that rhyme.

Animals Everywhere **159**

Writing and Grammar

Plan

 Talk about the animal you want to write a poem about.

Draw or **write** about the animal.

Choose an animal to write about.

_____

- -

_____

- -

_____

Tell what the animal can do.

_____

- -

_____

- -

_____

- -

_____

 Think about what words you might rhyme.

Writing and Grammar

Draft

Read Steve's draft of his poem.

Word Choice

My poem uses words that describe things.

A Tiger

I am a wild tiger,

I'm big and I'm strong,

My claws are big,

My tail is long!

I sleep in the day,

I hunt in the night,

Soon I will eat,

It's time for a bite!

Key Details

I included details in my poem.

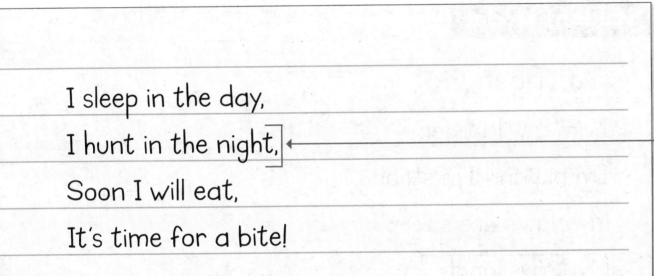

Your Turn

Begin to write your poem in your Writer's Notebook. Use your ideas from pages 160–161. Focus on descriptive words.

Writing and Grammar

Revise and Edit

Think about how Steve revised and edited his poem.

I revised by writing a better title.

I added details to make my poem more interesting.

Student Model

Go, **Tiger,** Go!

I am a wild tiger,

I'm big and I'm strong,

My claws are sharp,

My tail is long!

I spelled a word
with the long *e*
sound correctly.

I |sleep| in the day,

I hunt in the night,

|Soon| I will eat,

It's time for a bite!

I made sure to
use an adverb
that tells when
correctly.

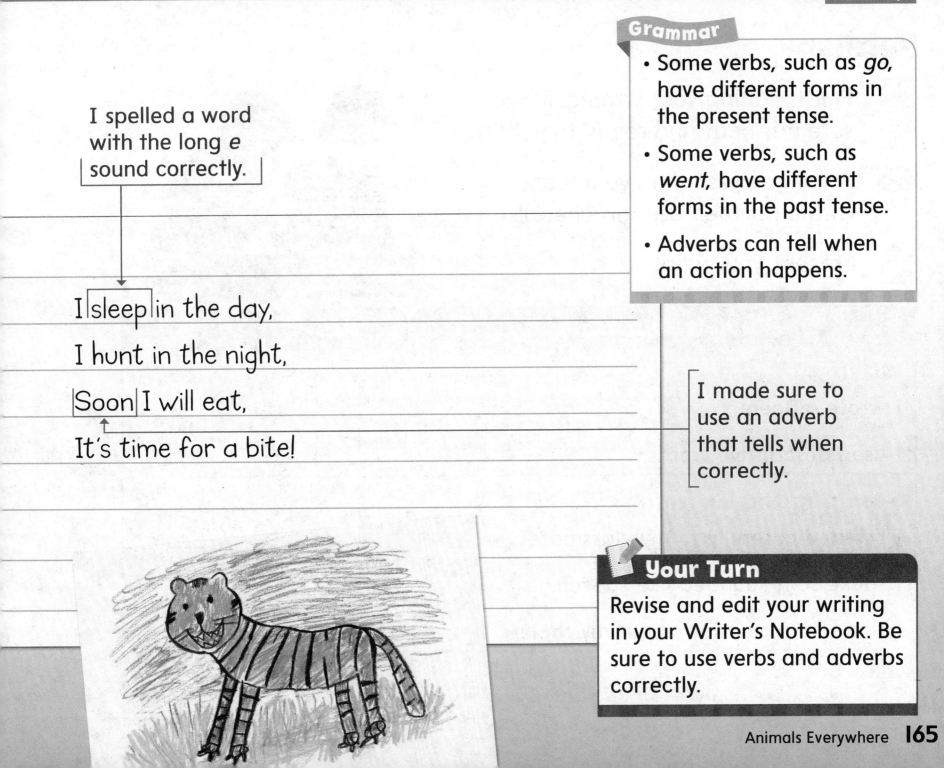

Your Turn

Revise and edit your writing in your Writer's Notebook. Be sure to use verbs and adverbs correctly.

Share and Evaluate

Publish

 Finish editing your writing. Make sure it is neat and ready to publish.

 Practice presenting your work with a partner. Use this checklist.

 Present your work.

Review Your Work	Yes	No
Writing		
I wrote a poem.	☐	☐
I used descriptive words.	☐	☐
Speaking and Listening		
I listened carefully to my classmates.	☐	☐
I spoke so it sounded like speech.	☐	☐
I shared information about my topic.	☐	☐

Talk with a partner about what you did well in your writing.

Write about your work.

What did you do well in your writing?

_____

- -

_____

- -

_____

What do you need to work on?

_____

- -

_____

- -

_____

Spiral Review

Genre:
• Folktale
• Nonfiction

Strategy:
• Visualize, Ask and Answer Questions

Skill:
• Sequence; Main Idea and Key Details

Vocabulary Strategy:
• Sentence Clues, Word Categories

Read "Little Red Hen." Use the illustrations to make images about the story in your mind.

Little Red Hen

Little Red Hen wanted to plant wheat.

"Who will help me?" she asked.

"Not I," replied Cow, Duck, and Pig.

Soon it was time to cut the wheat. "Who will help me?" asked Hen. "Not I," replied Cow, Duck, and Pig.

Then it was time to grind the wheat. "Who will help me?" asked Hen.

"Not I," replied Cow, Duck, and Pig.

Next, Little Red Hen baked bread with the wheat. The scent, or smell, was so good!

Cow, Duck, and Pig said, "We will help you eat the bread!"

"No, you will not!" said Little Red Hen. And she ate it all up.

Show What You Learned

Circle the correct answer to each question.

1 How do you know this story is a folktale?

   A The story has photos.
   B The story could happen in real life.
   C The animals speak and act like humans.

2 What does Little Red Hen do after she plants the wheat?

   A She cuts the wheat.
   B She eats the wheat.
   C She grinds the wheat.

3 What is the meaning of *scent* on page 169?

   A a type of bread
   B the way something smells
   C a coin

> **Quick Tip**
>
> Look at how a word is used in a sentence to figure out its meaning.

Read "Seals." Ask yourself questions about the text. Read to find the answers.

Seals

What animal lives on land and in the sea? A seal!

Most seals live in cold water along rocky coasts. In the daytime, they like to go on land. A seal uses its fins to get up on rocks. It may rest on the sand and soak up the sun.

A seal can slide on the ice on its fat belly. Its belly keeps the seal warm in the cold sea. That's where seals go to catch fish and shellfish to eat.

At the end of the day, seals go into the cold sea to sleep. A seal keep its heads out of water when it sleeps.

What animal lives on land and in the sea? A seal!

Circle the correct answer to each question.

1 How do you know this is nonfiction?

A It is a made-up story.
B It gives facts about real things.
C It tells a story about characters that do not exist in real life.

2 What is the main idea of the passage?

A Seals can live on land and in the sea.
B They like to sleep in the sea.
C They like to eat bananas.

3 What group of words in the text belong in the same category?

A sun, dive, coast
B sea, night, shellfish
C heads, fins, bellies

Quick Tip

Look at the photos when you reread text to help you answer the question.

Focus on Folktales

A **folktale** is a story that has been told for many, many years. It often has animal characters that speak and act like humans. A folktale can also have a message or lesson.

 Reread "Little Rabbit."

Talk with a partner about what makes this story a folktale.

Write about the lesson in this folktale. What does Little Rabbit learn?

_____

_____

_____

_____

_____

_____

_____

_____

_____

_____

_____

_____

_____

Share your ideas with your partner.

Respond to the Read Aloud

Remember, the **main idea** is what the text is about. **Key details** give information about the main idea.

 Listen to "Winter Warriors."

Talk about the key details of the selection.

Write the key details. Then write the main idea.

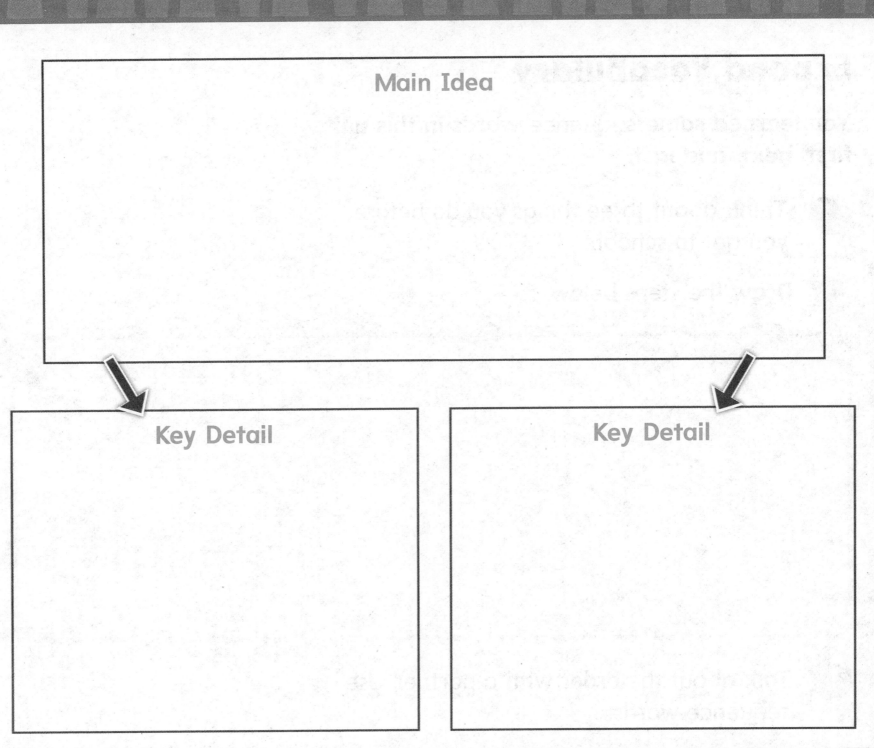

Main Idea

Key Detail

Key Detail

Expand Vocabulary

You learned some **sequence words** in this unit:
first, next, and **last.**

 Think about three things you do before
you get to school.

 Draw the steps below.

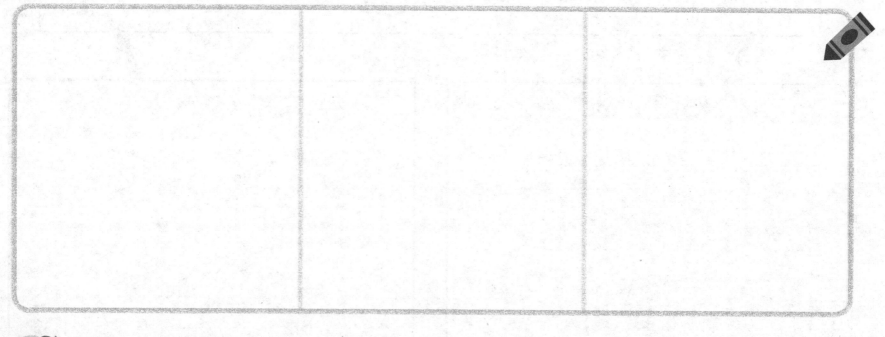

 Talk about the order with a partner. Use
sequence words.

Draw the steps for making a paper airplane.

 Tell a partner to follow the steps. Use *first, next,* and *last.* Have your partner repeat the steps out loud. Then take turns following the steps.

Extend Your Learning

Animal Report

You can use different sources to find information about a topic. Work with a partner to create a short report about an animal that lives in a jungle.

 Talk about the animal you want to learn about. Decide where to find information.

 Write the information below. You can also use a separate sheet of paper.

_____

- -

_____

- -

_____

 Share your work with the class.

Reading Digitally TIME FOR KIDS

Online texts sometimes have links that you can click on. Listen to "Teeth at Work" at my.mheducation.com. Click on the links.

 Talk about what happens when you click the first link.

 Write about the second link. What information does it give?

_____

_____

_____

_____

_____

_____

John Lund/Blend Images LLC

Extend Your Learning

Write a Poem

A **poem** often has short lines and may have rhythm.

 Look at and **think** about the poem below.

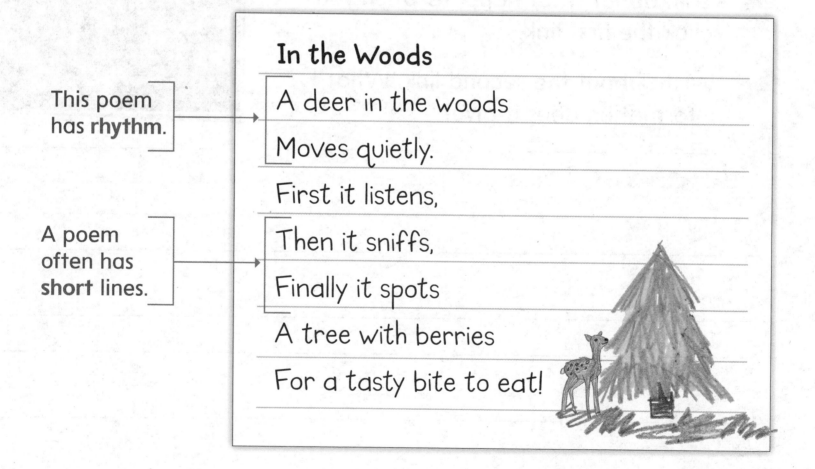

This poem has **rhythm**.

A poem often has **short** lines.

In the Woods

A deer in the woods

Moves quietly.

First it listens,

Then it sniffs,

Finally it spots

A tree with berries

For a tasty bite to eat!

Think about an animal you want to write a poem about.

 Write your poem below. Use short lines.

Choose Your Own Book

 Tell a partner about a book you want to read. Say why you want to read it.

 Write the title.

_____

- -

_____

 Write what you liked about the book. Tell your partner how it made you feel.

Minutes I Read

_____

- -

_____

_____

- -

_____

What Did You Learn?

Think about the skills you have learned.
How happy are you with what you can do?

I understand about main idea and key details.	🙂	😐	🙁
I understand point of view.	🙂	😐	🙁
I can use a dictionary.	🙂	😐	🙁
I understand word categories.	🙂	😐	🙁

What is something that you want to get better at?

_____

- -

_____

My Sound-Spellings

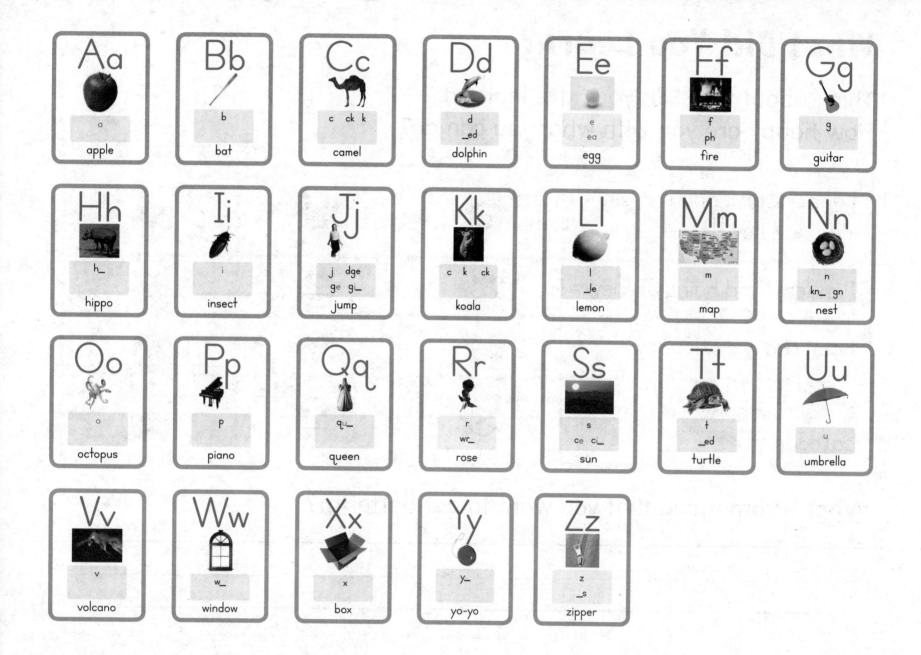

Aa a	**Bb** b	**Cc** c ck k	**Dd** d _ed	**Ee** e ea	**Ff** f ph	**Gg** g
apple	bat	camel	dolphin	egg	fire	guitar
Hh h_	**Ii** i	**Jj** j dge ge gi_	**Kk** c k ck	**Ll** l _le	**Mm** m	**Nn** n kn_ gn
hippo	insect	jump	koala	lemon	map	nest
Oo o	**Pp** p	**Qq** qu_	**Rr** r wr_	**Ss** s ce ci_	**Tt** t _ed	**Uu** u
octopus	piano	queen	rose	sun	turtle	umbrella
Vv v	**Ww** w_	**Xx** x	**Yy** y_	**Zz** z _s		
volcano	window	box	yo-yo	zipper		

th — thumb

sh — shell

ch / tch — cheese

wh_ — whale

ng — sing

a ai_ _ay / a_e ea ei — train

i y i_e / igh ie — five

o oa ow / o_e _oe — boat

u u_e / _ew _ue — cube

e_e ea ee / e _y / ie _ey — tree

ar — star

er ir / ur or — shirt

oar or ore — corn

ow / ou — cow

oi / _oy — boy

oo — book

oo u_e u / _ew ue / ou ui — spoon

a aw au / augh al — straw

air are / ear ere — chair

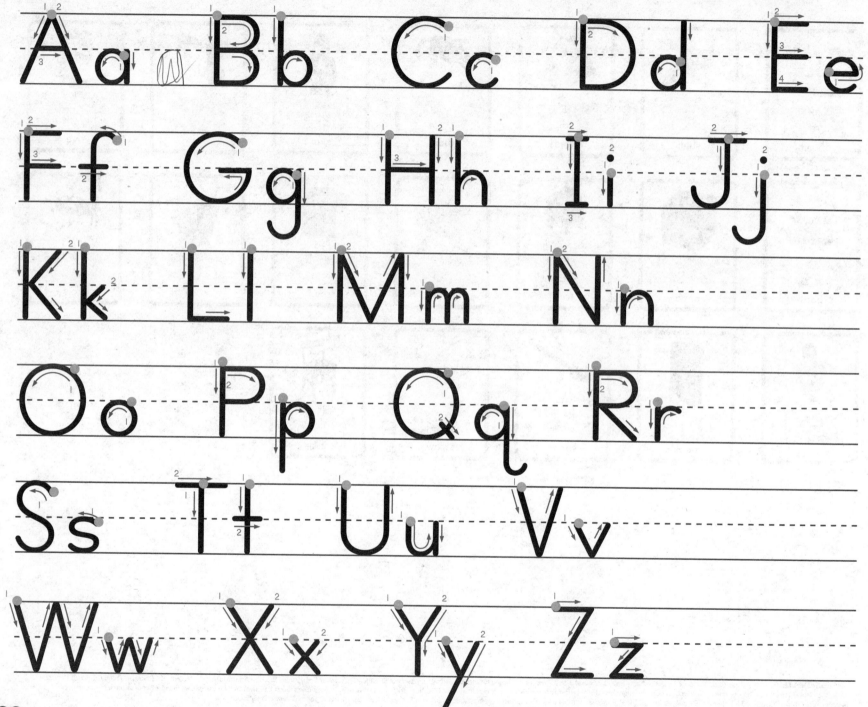

1. Love ?
2.
3.
4.
5.
6.
7.